BLACK INCOME SHIFTERS

Shift Your Cashflow From Red To Black

RICK HOPKINS & ODESSA HOPKINS

ISBN: 978-0-9855552-6-9

Book Cover Design & Layout by PIXEL eMarketing INC.

Legal Disclaimer

FOREWORD

People who work hard every day, earn a decent income and provide for themselves and their families should expect to live comfortably in America. We are the wealthiest country on Earth, accounting for 25% of the world's total wealth. Yet, 80% of us are struggling financially, 69% have less than $1,000 in savings, and only 4% are able to retire someday without having to lower their standard of living. The problem isn't that you don't earn enough money; most likely, it's that you don't have full access to the money you already make. In this book, *Rick and Odessa Hopkins* make you aware that someone is getting rich off your money; unfortunately, that someone probably isn't you.

Taxes take the first third of your income and revolving debt takes the next third. The reason you can't get ahead is that you are trying to make ends meet on only the remaining third of your income. Contrary to popular belief, the solution to this problem is not to work longer hours or take on a second job. In many cases this approach will only make matters worse, i.e. the law of diminishing returns. The authors will introduce you to a concept called *"Income Shifting"* that will give you strategies to defeat your two greatest financial enemies: the taxman and the banker.

Ours is a capitalistic economy. In its purest form, you will either capitalize on others or be capitalized yourself. Capitalism is driven by private business and investments. The key to building wealth in this environment requires diversification of income. You can't earn all of your income from a job. You must also incorporate the tax advantages of 1099 and investment income. Income Shifting allows employees to access tax advantages formerly available only to traditional business owners and investors; then shows you how to strategically utilize new cashflow from tax savings to eliminate debt and invest. It is time to actively *participate* in capitalism as a producer; not just *contribute* to it as a consumer.

"Thank you Rick and Odessa Hopkins for these insights, gems and nuggets of brilliance. You have put your time, talent and treasure into this important book. I was not only informed and inspired, but empowered by your commitment, words and ideas on this critical element of capitalism particularly in the Black community. Economics is the New Black Power. Your insights into *"Income Shifting"* will most certainly help us all close the income and wealth gap. My heartfelt thanks goes out to the Hopkins for providing us all a clear way to help manifest our financial destiny. Read this important gem.

Dr. George C. Fraser
Author, *Success Runs In Our Race*

ABOUT THE AUTHOR

Rick Hopkins took early retirement after thirty years as a senior executive with our country's largest nonprofit organization. His interest and demonstrated skill in the areas of finance and fiscal management led him to found **RH Consulting**, a Washington DC area based cashflow management consulting firm. After several years as an entrepreneur, Hopkins was called out of retirement in 2013 to take on a special assignment overseeing the construction and operation of a new program facility in a New York City beach community devastated by Hurricane Sandy.

Hopkins is an Amazon #1 Best Selling author with four publications to his credit. He and his wife, Odessa, founded **Black Income Shifters** in 2016, a financial education and economic empowerment company based in New York City.

Odessa Hopkins brings 20 years of onsite federal government contracting to her portfolio with Technology & Management Services (TMS) and, later, IBM. During her onsite career, she quadrupled contracting tasks and revenue

Odessa has been an entrepreneur since the mid 1980s but, in 2007, she launched Another Approach Enterprises, a business and diversity consulting company that assists start-ups to large corporations: one of which exceeds $11B a year in annual revenue. In addition, she is the Creator of BizWomenOnline.com and Co-Founder of Black Income Shifters.

CONTENTS

ENTREPRENEURIAL SPIRIT

"In every success story, you
will find someone who made a
courageous decision."

PETER F. DRUCKER

True entrepreneurs identify a problem, then solve it. The problem Odessa and I have identified is that people are trying to live on only a third of their hard earned salary. Income taxes take the first third and interest on debt takes the second; for most people, the remaining third is simply not enough to make ends meet. Working longer hours, taking on a second job or changing to a career that pays better seems like a good move, right? Maybe not. I believe the solution to your problem can be found in the money you already make.

If you are an employee who pays too much in taxes and needs to get out of debt, and who wants to stop living paycheck to paycheck and free up more cashflow to pay bills and invest; you have come to the right place. Our capitalistic economy is built on *private business* and *investing*. If you are not involved with both, or either, you are not _participating_ in capitalism… you are just _contributing_ your hard-earned money to it.

Uncle Sam definitely plays favorites; and he prefers producers to consumers. If you are participating in capitalism, you are considered to be a *producer*; if not, you are just a *consumer*, good only for buying stuff and paying taxes. He sees producers as *financial partners* who help him grow the economy. The evidence is in the tax codes. He sees employees as financial cannon fodder and charges you the highest possible tax rates while allowing you the fewest tax deductions.

This is no different than his preference for *homeowners* over *renters*. He rewards homeowners with tax deductions, credits and other tax advantages. Homeowners get the *elevator* while renters get the *shaft*. There are many more employees than business owners and many more renters than homeowners. Shouldn't the majority get a break? Well, if you are looking for fairness, the tax codes are not the place to find it.

Instead, look to financial education. The financial world, like everything else, has *rules of engagement*. Make the effort to learn and apply them in your life; but more importantly, teach your loved ones to do the same. This process is the foundation for creating and perpetuating generational wealth in our families and communities.

Financial Rules Of Engagement

The wealthy teach their kids differently than the rest of us. The middle class teaches their kids to get a degree, find a good job with benefits, and retire in 40 years with a gold watch. The wealthy teach their kids not just to <u>have</u> a job; but to <u>own</u> their job. Get your degree, yes; find a good job, certainly; but don't stop there. Learn all there is to know about that job; then start a business and invest your profits. This is capitalism at work.

To actually *participate* in capitalism, you need to be in business at some level and be an investor. There are many ways to be in business other than the traditional model of leasing a building, hiring staff and dealing with operational and legal issues. It is the same with investing. How much you invest is less important than whether or not you do so consistently. Compound interest is a beautiful thing.

This book was written with the wage earning W2 employee in mind. *Did you know that over 90% of employees earn 100% of their income from a job?* Whatever happened to "don't put all your eggs in one basket?" That was excellent advice, by the way. What happens if you lose your job? What is your "Plan B?" The average employee has no answer for these questions; and therein, as they say, lies the rub.

Income Shifting is the answer. It levels the financial playing field for the W2 employee. Income Shifting is *the process of shifting your income from the highest tax bracket to the lowest, utilizing the tax advantages of homebased business and investments to mitigate the downsides of W2 job income.* The beauty of it all is that you are creating new cashflow from the money you already make.

The Sword And The Shield

Income Shifting allows for a number of, what I like to call, *Sword & Shield Strategies.* Imagine a gladiator, fighting for his life in the coliseums of ancient Rome. He would have a sword, his primary weapon; and a shield, a back up weapon, to protect his life. Your job is like a gladiator's sword, it is your primary income source; *your homebased business is like a shield that protects your job income from excessive taxation.*

I believe that the entrepreneurial spirit that built this country and made it great needs to be revitalized. That sense of rugged individualism seems to have been diminished by the industrial revolution and the flood of young people leaving home to work at factories and businesses in the big cities. We have become narrowly focused specialists, and function like replaceable cogs in someone else's machinery.

With the advance of technology and the *Information Age*, many low skill, high paying jobs began to disappear. Lacking job skills, the entrepreneurial spirit of our forefathers, and diverse multiple streams of income; our dependence on social programs increased across the board. *Income Shifting* represents a viable alternative strategy for the everyday wage earning W2 employee to not just survive in the new economy... but thrive in it.

CHAPTER 1

TAKE HOME WHAT YOU MAKE HOME

"You must pay taxes, but there's no law that says that you have to leave a tip."

UNKNOWN

What is *Income Shifting*? It is not a new or original concept. It has been used by the wealthy for generations to shelter their valuable assets from taxation. It has been common practice to transfer valuable assets, such as real estate, into the names of minor children in order to pay less tax. While this practice may seem a little "sketchy" to some, it is quite legal. Where tax law is concerned, you will often struggle with *right and wrong* versus *legal and illegal*.

Those of us without lots of valuable assets to protect can also use a *variation* of the *Income Shifting* strategy above effectively. However, it certainly requires a thorough understanding of money, and how it really works in America. For example, there are basically three ways that income is earned in this country:

1. *W2 Income* (Job)

2. *1099 Income* (Business)

3. *Investment Income*

Each revenue stream has its own advantages and disadvantages; and its own tax rate as well. *W2 employees pay the highest tax rate and are allowed the fewest tax deductions.* While 1099 business owners pay less than W2s as a result of being taxed only on what is left over after expenses; as well as, being allowed hundreds of business tax deductions not available to employees.

Investment income may just be the best deal of all. It is taxed at only about half the rate of W2 income. You should be starting to see a pattern here. Money making money is always taxed less than labor making money. The wealthy operate in the realm of business and investments; while the majority of wage earning employees depend *exclusively* on a job.

Shift Your Mindset, Shift Your Income

Armed with this information we can now begin to design an *Income Shifting* strategy "for the rest of us." For our purposes, *Income Shifting* means: *"To shift your income from the highest tax bracket to the lowest, utilizing the tax advantages of homebased business ownership to lower income taxes and debt while building investment income."*

In other words, we must learn how to create *positive cashflow* by shifting job income through a part time homebased business, maximizing the tax advantages of business ownership and minimizing the downsides of W2 income; ultimately, freeing up money for investment and asset acquisition. This sounds more complicated than it really is; but by the end of this book, you will be an old pro.

Income Shifting is an *employee based strategy*, so let's begin on familiar ground for all employees, your paycheck! Without the tax advantages afforded business owners, such as paying tax only on money left over after expenses are paid and the hundreds of tax deductions; or the 50% lower income tax rate charged to investments… it's no wonder employees end up struggling from paycheck to paycheck.

Imagine that your <u>net</u> pay at work mirrored your <u>gross</u> pay… would that change your life? An employee who earns $50,000 a year, will only take home around $35,000… primarily due to federal income taxes. How many bills could you pay with that $15,000 of *your own money* in <u>your</u> pocket instead of Uncle Sam's?

Please, don't misunderstand me. *I don't condone income tax evasion.* I believe in paying every penny one owes in taxes… but not a penny more. However, what you actually "owe" under IRS tax code is a fluid concept. The amount you actually owe *before* taking advantage of the many legal loopholes that exist in our voluminous tax codes will be much lower *afterwards*.

Allow me to demonstrate with this, admittedly, over-simplified example. The three scenarios are for illustrative purposes only:

1. A W2 employee earns $50,000 a year, and is taxed up front on each dollar earned... approximately $15,000.

2. A business owner also earns $50,000; but spends $40,000 operating his business. He writes off his expenses as business deductions; as a result, his tax is on $10,000... approximately $3,000.

3. A W2 employee with a homebased business earns $50,000 on the job. He also earns $5,000 with his homebased business, but spends $20,000 operating it... showing a business loss of $15,000 on paper. He applies the $15,000 business loss to his $50,000 W2 income and now pays income taxes on $35,000... approximately $10,000.

Did you know that income tax was never supposed to be permanent? It was invoked in

1862, and was intended to be a *temporary measure* to help support the Civil War effort—and it just never went away! Actually, that's not true; it did go away for a couple of years. In 1895 the US Supreme Court actually ruled federal income tax to be unconstitutional; but it didn't take long for Uncle Sam to overturn that ruling and get his sticky fingers back in our wallets.

Once again, if you are looking for *fairness*, the tax codes are not the place to find it. *It's a fact that even though the wealthy make more money, they pay proportionately less in taxes.* This doesn't happen by accident; the wealthy are purposeful in their efforts to minimize their taxable income. You should do the same. Income shifting simply takes advantage of *existing tax laws* to allow W2 employees a fighting chance to keep more of what they earn and begin to build assets and generational wealth.

The Magic Of The W4

You are probably familiar with the **W4 Tax Withholding Form**. You filled one out when you got your first job… and every other job since then. Did you know that, according to the IRS, over 80% of Americans fill this form out incorrectly; causing too much tax to be withheld from their paychecks? This is not surprising, however; since employers, by law, are not allowed to instruct you on how to properly fill out this form.

The most an employer will tell you when asked what an "allowance" is; or how many allowances you should claim is *just claim zero or one so that you don't owe any tax at the end of the year.*" To say that this is bad advice is an understatement; but millions blindly follow it for their entire working career... leaving thousands of dollars a year of their own money on the table. Perhaps when you were sixteen, living at home, with no spouse or dependents claiming zero or one made sense; now, not so much.

The main problem is that people generally aren't clear on the definition of "allowance." Contrary to popular belief, an allowance is not the same as a *dependent* or an *exemption. An allowance is a mathematical calculation that determines how much money your employer will withhold from your pay check.* The number is not etched in stone and will change as situations in your life change.

Properly utilized, the W4 is a beautiful thing. It can be a veritable *payment gateway,* allowing a fast and efficient means for Uncle Sam to return your hard-earned tax money to your monthly paycheck. *It is preferable to a tax refund where Uncle Sam holds your money for a year, uses it to pay his bills and invest, then returns it to you without paying you any interest.* Oh, and to add insult to injury, he unashamedly taxes it before returning it to you!

According to the IRS, the average amount of a tax refund is $2,000 to $4,000 a year. Wouldn't it be better for you to have use of your own money all year to pay your own bills, lower your credit card or other debt, and perhaps begin a modest investment program? I am not going to waste my breath convincing some people that a tax refund is not a good thing… either you get it or you don't. If you don't, then you won't get income shifting, either.

Know Your Enemy

Keeping more of your own money is fundamental. Every credible wealth building strategy begins with minimizing your taxes. It is a simple matter of awareness. In his book, THE ART OF WAR, Sun Tzu says: "Know the enemy and know yourself and in a hundred battles you will be victorious." Surely, you could not expect to defeat a formidable enemy without knowing his strengths and weaknesses; and how they match up to your own.

I would take Sun Tzu's advice a step further. You

cannot hope to defeat an enemy that you do not even know exists. When I speak and train on the subject of Income Shifting, I usually start out with a seemingly straightforward question: "What is your largest monthly expense?" Participants quickly and confidently answer "my rent" or "my mortgage." They are quite surprised to find out that they are wrong. Almost to a person, their largest expense is income taxes; that's right, good ole' Uncle Sam!

We have been paying so much tax for so long that we are, literally, numb to it. You lose a third of your income to income taxes, right off the top. If you count sales taxes, property taxes and other specialty taxes, it's over 50%. This is true for employees, but not necessarily for business owners. Why are tax laws biased against employees? Think about it. The lawmakers you send to Washington to presumably represent *your* interests… are they employees or business owners?

We all complain about high taxes, of course; but seem consigned to the belief that there is nothing we can do about it. The wealthy complain as well; the difference is that they do something about it… up to and including buying politicians and lawmakers to create loopholes in the tax laws. Unlike many of us, they do not go gently into that good night.

Okay, now you are aware of *Financial Enemy #1, the Taxman*. Now that you know he exists, we can develop a financial battle plan to defeat him. I wish I could say that taxes were the only financial enemy holding you back; unfortunately, there are three more that we must also defeat along the way. You will meet them in the next couple of chapters.

Your Other Financial Enemies

In the next chapters, I will introduce three additional obstacles that make it difficult, if not impossible, for wage earners to attain financial success in our community:

- Financial Enemy #2: *Interest Debt*
- Financial Enemy #3: *Inflation*
- Financial Enemy #4: *Inadequate Cashflow Management*

Each adversary requires its own strategy, or battle plan, to defeat it. It is worth your while to become familiar with the *financial rules of engagement* before taking on these very formidable financial adversaries.

NOTES

CHAPTER 2

I OWE, I OWE
IT'S OFF TO WORK I GO

"The borrower is the slave of the lender."

PROVERBS 22:7

Financial Enemy #2 is *Debt*; specifically, debt resulting from payments on interest. Examples include credit cards, automobile loans, mortgages, student loans, etc. Debt takes the second third of your income. *As with government and business, a symbiotic relationship also exists between debt and taxes.* They feed off each other.

Ironically, people find themselves in *debt* as a result of attempts to compensate for the money lost to *taxes* with credit cards and other high interest loans. Just as taxes are Uncle Sam's primary revenue source, *interest* is where banks make most of their money. This is why they are so over the top with bank fees.

Interest charges, large and small, are built into all services provided by financial institutions. The silver lining in this cloud is that interest, unlike tax, is a completely *voluntary* expense. You are not required by law to take out credit cards or borrow money. It may seem like a good idea at the time; but can often make matters worse instead of better.

However, managing your debt *does* require you to make some tough choices; and not always a choice between good and bad. Sometimes the choice is between the lesser of two evils, as illustrated by the following:

> *A hit man took his victim to the edge of a cliff, put a gun to his head and told him "Jump or I will blow your head off." The victim sighed and said, "I guess I don't have a choice." The hit man snickered and said, "of course you have a choice... just not a very good one!"*

What we buy and borrow is too often driven by *ego* rather than *intellect*. How many times have you heard someone brag about how much they spent for an expensive home or automobile? In sales, there is a technique called *"selling them their ego."* Make it all about them and they will buy. Playing to the ego is extremely effective in closing the sale. Don't go for the "old okey-doke."

Our salary is yet another area where *ego* can override *intellect*. Our feeling of self-worth is sometimes tied to how much we make. If an employee's salary is $50,000 a year, we realize that he doesn't actually take home all $50,000. Roughly $15,000 will go to income taxes, right off the top. Yet, we feel better about ourselves at $50,000 than at $35,000. The problem is, however, that we still spend $50,000.

Bankers don't hesitate to take full advantage of this prevailing emotional flaw. Think about the last time you applied for a mortgage, or auto loan, or even a credit card. You were *qualified* based on your gross salary, not what you actually take home. Using the example above, our person would qualify based on $50,000, not $35,000. The repayment schedule would be based on $50,000 of actual income, not $35,000. Where is that extra $15,000 supposed to come from?

"I Will Gladly Pay You Tuesday For A Hamburger Today"

For those of you who do not remember; or perhaps who may not have been born yet, that famous quote is by a character named *Wimpy* from the old *Popeye the Sailor* cartoons of my youth. Wimpy loved hamburgers, but he was always broke. Because he had no money, Wimpy would constantly try to borrow money from his friends to buy a hamburger with the promise that he would pay them back next Tuesday.

I assume that Wimpy must have had a job, although it was never mentioned; and that Tuesday was his payday. In retrospect, it was a moot point as no one ever lent him any money anyway. But what if credit cards had been around back then? If so, how much debt do you suppose Wimpy would have found himself in due to his lack of financial discipline?

Wimpy would be right at home today because we have become a society that would gladly pay you next Tuesday for pretty much anything if they can have what they want today. So what if you end up paying for it many times over because you are unable to keep up with agreed upon payments? What good is it to be able to buy a Jaguar... but also have to sleep in it?

You can _choose_ not to swipe that credit card because you know full well that you don't have enough money in your checking account. You can _choose_ to redirect money you now spend on _liabilities_ and apply it to acquiring _assets_. But the most impactful choice you can make is to _choose_ to _educate yourself financially_, regarding how to pay less in taxes, get out of debt and free up money to invest and acquire assets..

Educating yourself is only the first step. Implementing what you have learned is the second. But passing this knowledge on to your children and loved ones is your ultimate objective. Paying it forward in this manner is the foundation of how the wealthy build *generational wealth*; and is a model we should all emulate.

Death By A Thousand Cuts

Financial Enemy #3 is Inflation. Inflation is simply the rising cost of living. Every year, things are going to cost more. It is sometimes referred to as *Death by a Thousand Cuts* because it just eats away at your income bit by bit, day after day, week after week, month after month, year after year. The annual rate of inflation usually fluctuates between 2% and 4% a year; which doesn't seem like a lot in the grand scheme of things.

What we often fail to realize is that the effects of inflation are cumulative. A 3% increase in inflation last year, when coupled with another 3% increase this year is actually 6%. If it goes up again 3% next year, then you are at 9% and counting. Don't wait until the numbers get into double digits before you take corrective action.

Rising inflation, however, is not the problem. The real problem is that employee incomes have not been keeping pace with inflation; primarily due to a practice known as *salary suppression*. Retired seniors are not the only ones on fixed incomes. Employees are also limited in how much they are allowed to get paid. Salary suppression makes it extremely difficult to outpace inflation.

Did you know that the rate of inflation doubles every twenty years or so in this country? If twenty years ago you were making $30,000 in salary, and today you are making $60,000... I regret to inform you that, in *buying power*, you are still only making $30,000! If you haven't doubled your salary in the last 20 years, you have failed to keep up with inflation.

Banks Are A Sucker's Bet

For the record, putting money in a bank savings account is NOT a recommended financial strategy. Why? Because the bank will pay you less interest than the rate of inflation. In other words, *the interest paid is so low that your money is guaranteed to be worth less when you take it out than when you put it in!* Thanks to inflation, banking your money isn't much better off than stuffing it in a mattress or burying it in the back yard! So what is the alternative?

Let's take a look at what happens to your money when you deposit it at your local bank. Your money is guaranteed by FDIC Insurance, but it doesn't just sit there in the bank vault, safe and sound, waiting for you to return for it. Your money is out the door even before you are; on its way to making someone other than you rich.

The banks immediately invest your funds with money management companies like Vanguard, Fidelity and T. Rowe Price, where they typically will earn 8%, to 12% interest. The banks will then pay you 1% or 2% interest on your savings and then pocket the rest. The irony is that wage earners have the option to invest their personal funds directly with those exact same money management companies.

I get it… you were taught that saving and investing your money was best left to the professionals. I agree, to an extent; but not every financial decision needs a CPA. *Why not skip the middleman sometimes, and earn those higher interest rates yourself?* This is one simple way to outpace inflation. Is there risk? Of course; but it is manageable risk. Without some amount of risk, it is impossible to build wealth.

Let's do the math. If the bank earns a modest 6% on your money and then pays you 1% interest; what is the net percent of interest earned by the bank? The obvious answer would be 5%, right? Wrong! The net percentage earned by the bank was not 5%; the percentage was, in fact, _infinite_ because they risk *your* money, not *theirs*! Think about it. How much does it cost you when someone else loses money?

Welcome to capitalism. Don't hate the player, _learn_ the game. If you don't know the financial rules of engagement, how can you possibly expect to win the game... or even compete for that matter? It may not seem like a game, but it is... and money is how you keep score.

NOTES

_____

_____

_____

_____

_____

_____

_____

_____

_____

_____

_____

_____

_____

_____

_____

_____

CHAPTER 3

CASHFLOW MANAGEMENT 101

"Cashflow is created by the decisions you
make with the money you earn."

RICK HOPKINS

Financial Enemy #4 is *Inadequate Cashflow Management*. Cashflow and income are simply not the same thing. *Cashflow is created by the decisions you make with the money you earn.* Cashflow is not a noun, it is a *verb*... at least it should be. It is an action word, comprised of the money you earn, save, borrow, leverage, invest, etc.

We all aspire to what is known as *financial success*. This is where you have enough cashflow to live your desired lifestyle now; and still put aside enough to retire someday without having to lower your standard of living. That doesn't seem like so much to ask, does it? However, instead of *financial success*, most of us are locked into a cycle of *financial failure*.

Financial failure occurs when your lack of money costs you money. It is when you are forced to swipe that credit card for necessities because you simply don't have enough cash. Financial failure is when you have to decide which creditors get paid this month, and which ones have to wait. Prolonged exposure to financial failure results in a condition I call the

Cycle of Pain. The symptoms are unfortunate, but easy to recognize:

1. You have no money
2. You are in debt
3. You have no savings or investments

Financial failure is not preordained. It can be mitigated with a consistent regimen of financial education supplemented with a liberal dose of entrepreneurial spirit. It is that same entrepreneurial spirit that built this country; and the lack of which has transformed us into a nation of employees. Financial failure is like moving through dangerous territory; you want to keep it moving... don't pitch a tent and stay there.

Managing your cashflow is a moot point if you have no cashflow to manage, so where do you find it? After all, you are barely making ends meet as it is. Good news... you can find the money you need in the money you *already make*! Unless you have a gambling or substance abuse problem, or catastrophic medical issues, you probably make enough money to be comfortable. The problem is that you are losing two thirds of what you make to the *taxman* and the *banker*... and most of the rest to your other two financial enemies.

RICK HOPKINS & ODESSA HOPKINS

My father used to tell me that the best place to look for lost money is in the same place you lost it. For most people, that place is taxes. This book exposes you to financial strategies that allow you to "take back your tax" from good old Uncle Sam. You learn how to use that new cashflow to eliminate your debt. Savings from taxes and debt can then be used to establish an emergency fund and to begin a strategic investment program.

Generational wealth does not happen by accident. Financial education must be learned and passed down within families and communities over time. Economic empowerment does not come from the public schools, or the government or from your employer; it comes when *each one teaches one.*

Each One Teach Two

When my wife and I founded our new company, **Black Income Shifters**, we readily acknowledged that our community is starting out from behind. Therefore we adopted the mantra *"Each one teach one is no longer good enough... each one teach two."* Let's all work together to level the financial playing field for all, and address the disproportionate distribution of wealth in this country by educating ourselves and the ones we love.

We were inspired by the teachings of Mr. Ivey Stokes, founder of Atlanta based financial services company, myEcon, Inc. Mr. Stokes espouses the concept of *Personal Financial Success*; and breaks down complex financial strategies in such a way that anyone can understand them. His construct of identifying the four major obstacles to financial success and the three solutions is the basis for the *Income Shifters Academy*.

Behavioral psychologists suggest that it takes twenty one days to form a lasting habit. The Academy begins with twenty one days of intense, concentrated financial education. The curriculum consists of training videos, reading assignments and real world field assignments where you earn real money, write off real expenses and make real investments.

Three complimentary 30-minute personal coaching sessions are provided just in case you need a little additional support. The Academy founders are both experienced *cashflow management consultants*, and are available for scheduled appointments. I recommend that you use your coaching sessions as needed for accountability, and to help keep you on track.

The Academy workflow allows you to move at your own pace from the comfort and convenience of home. The important thing is that you complete the curriculum, and that you internalize the financial education and strategies.

The *Academy* goal is for you to emerge a master of creating new cashflow from the money you already make, shifting that cashflow from the highest tax bracket to the lowest, and managing your cashflow with maximum efficiency. Then pay it forward by teaching two other people what you have learned… each one teach two.

It can be done.

NOTES

CHAPTER 4

THREE STEPS TO FINANCIAL SUCCESS

"He who fails to plan, plans to fail."

BENJAMIN FRANKLIN

A T this point we have identified the financial enemies of your success. They are *Taxes, Debt, Inflation* and *Inadequate Cashflow Management*. Now it is time to introduce you to three counter strategies that will allow you to overcome these obstacles. I call them the **Three Steps To Financial Success**. They are:

1. Income Shifting
2. Business Ownership
3. Build Investment Income

Right now your money is busy making *somebody* rich; unfortunately, that somebody probably is not you. Given this, your first strategic objective should be to *take back control of your own money*. There are lots of obstacles preventing you from doing this. Your two most formidable adversaries are *high taxes* and *interest debt*; this is why we have to deal with them on the front end.

STEP ONE: Income shifting

Income Shifting means *to shift your income from the highest tax bracket to the lowest, utilizing the tax advantages of homebased business ownership to minimize income taxes and debt, while building investment income.*

Employees get the short end of the stick. They are taxed *up front*, pay the highest tax rate and get the fewest tax deductions. Business owners pay a lower rate due to paying income tax only on what is left over *after expenses*; as well as access to hundreds of tax deductions. Investors, on the other hand, pay the lowest tax rate possible, approximately half of what employees pay.

Income shifting allows employees to level the financial playing field, and begins the process of taking back your hard-earned tax dollars from Uncle Sam; but it doesn't stop there. Once you have begun to create new cashflow from tax savings you should have a plan for how best to use it. Never allow it to mingle with your other funds in your bill paying accounts. Before you realize, it will be gone without a trace.

If taxes are taking the first third of your income and debt is taking another third, then using your tax savings to eliminate debt seems like a logical strategy to me. Even just a couple of hundred dollars monthly from tax savings combined with your usual credit card payment each month, will often pay off that card in a few months instead of a few years.

And wouldn't it feel awfully good to pay off that auto loan in just two years instead of five... and to put three years of car payments in your 401k? The genius of income shifting is that it allows you to create new streams of income with the money you already make.

The secret to wealth building is in the *strategic* use of your own money. It is not always about earning more money; sometimes it is about making less of the money you already earn taxable. This allows you to keep more of your own money, and provides additional cashflow that will be helpful as you implement the *Three Steps To Financial Success*.

The W4 Gateway

The W4 is gateway to our *Income Shifting* strategy because it starts the tax savings ball rolling for W2 employees and wage earners. *According to the IRS, over 80% of Americans have too much income tax withheld from their paychecks because they filled out their W4 incorrectly.* How do you know if you are one of the 80%? Simple. If you get a tax refund every year, you are one of the 80%.

The average tax refund is between $2,000 and $4,000 a year. Could you use another $200 to $500 in your paycheck every month? The W4 allows you to get that money in your paycheck to pay bills, lower debt and invest; instead of waiting a year for a tax refund that pays you no interest on your money.

Once you begin to see that extra money in your paycheck, it feels like giving yourself a raise without working longer hours, getting a second job, or begging your boss for a raise. You are in control. You tell your employer how much tax to withhold, not the other way around. You decide whether to increase or decrease your allowances based on what is happening in your life.

Sadly, many people work their entire career without understanding their *W4 Tax Withholding Form*. They don't know that it is two pages long, or that it has three different worksheets that can be used to calculate allowances, as well as the *Employee's Withholding Allowance Certificate*. You are probably more familiar with the latter. This is where you put the number of allowances you plan to claim.

If more people understood the worksheets, the common practice of *"just claim zero or one so that you won't owe tax at the end of the year"* could finally be debunked. The worksheets will instruct you on how many allowances apply to you and your specific situation. It is not an exact science, but it works pretty well. And don't forget to make changes to your W4 allowances as significant tax related changes occur in your life.

On page one, you will find the *Personal Allowances Worksheet*. If you read and honestly answer all questions on this worksheet, it would be extremely difficult to claim only "zero or one." For example:

> *A single mother of two who claimed the Child Care Credit might assume that her number would be 3… one for herself and one for each of her dependents. My experience with similar cases has been that, depending on her individual circumstances, she would actually qualify for twice or even three times that number. Conversely, a single man with no dependents and no mortgage interest would be hard-pressed to exceed two allowances.*

At this point, people assume they are finished, but there are still two more worksheets to go on page two. I believe that the placement of the *Employee's Withholding Allowance Certificate* on page one instead of page two encourages this misunderstanding.

There are lots of potential allowances waiting for you on page two... assuming that you have a mortgage or a homebased business. Not everyone can afford to take on a home mortgage; but you can get into a homebased business for the cost of a pair of Jordans!

This is a perfect segue to the next step, where we outline the extremely favorable tax advantages of having a homebased business working in conjunction with your job. It is a one, two combination that is hard to beat. We are not finished with the W4, though; it will play a big part in *Step Two* as well.

STEP TWO: Business Ownership

The path to wealth in our capitalistic society leads through *business ownership, investments and asset acquisition*. It is like not believing in the Devil. Just because you don't believe in him, doesn't mean he doesn't exist. Business and investing drive capitalism. Believe it or not, it is true. If you aren't involved with either, I would ask you, "How is that working for you?"

Let's face it, not everyone is cut out to be a

traditional business owner; in fact, most would fail. Renting and operating a facility, dealing with human resources and legal issues, etc. can be intimidating. This is why every employee should, instead, avail themselves of the tax advantages of having a homebased business.

Homebased business allows you access to the same tax deductions available to traditional business owners, and allows you to *participate* in capitalism as a producer; not just *contribute* to it as a consumer. To qualify, you need dedicate only three to four hours a week to working your business with the *intent* to make a profit. It's okay if it takes some time to become profitable.

Business ownership, even just part time, is an excellent strategy for dealing with *Financial Enemy #1: Excessive Taxation.* Uncle Sam plays favorites. He clearly prefers business owners to employees. Nowhere are his preferences more evident than in the tax codes. He shows his preferences in the guise of tax deductions. Business owners get the elevator and employees get the shaft.

Business ownership allows employees to implement what I refer to as a *Sword and Shield* financial strategy. Envision an ancient gladiator battling for his life in a Roman coliseum. He would have a sword for attack and a shield for defense. His mighty sword would be his primary weapon. His shield protected his life should his primary weapon fail.

Your job is like a gladiator's sword. It is your primary source of income. It pays your bills, feeds, clothes and houses your family. *Your homebased business functions as your shield.* It protects your W2 job income from excessive taxation. Sometimes, a gladiator's sword is just not enough and needs the support of his shield. Similarly, sometimes your job alone just doesn't cut it... that's where your homebased business comes in.

Owning a homebased business gives you two distinct advantages over employees:

1. Business Tax Deductions
2. 1099 Business Income

In general, 1099 business income comes directly or indirectly from the sale of products and services. Anecdotally, only 20% of people will excel at generating 1099 business income. Why? Because people hate to sell stuff. The remaining 80% will do a much better job of creating new cashflow through strategic claiming of business tax deductions.

It is imminently possible for employees to capitalize on the tax advantages of a homebased business without a lot of selling and recruiting? Most companies won't tell you this, however, because company profits are based primarily on the sale of products and services. You can definitely build wealth without a lot of selling and recruiting; however, it will take longer.

Converting everyday expenses into lucrative business tax deductions is the secret sauce that makes this possible. *The key is to write off expenses you were going to spend money on anyway.* For example, you need your cell phone, laptop, meals, internet, car, travel and home office to run your business. With a little effort and creativity, you can justify writing off most of your everyday expenses to your business.

Remember when I mentioned that we were not finished with the W4? Well here we go again. *The W4 allows you to convert your business tax deductions into allowances that can put even more money into your paycheck each month.* This conversion occurs on Page 2 of the W4.

Simply put, every $4,050 dollars in business expense converts to one allowance. As a frame of reference, I typically generate from $20,000 to

$25,000 in business expenses every year… resulting in four or five additional allowances on my W4. The tax laws can be a beautiful thing!

Profits Are Better Than Wages

The ability to generate *1099 business income* is still an integral part of the Business Ownership Strategy. When employees need extra income the first options that usually come to mind are working longer hours or getting a second job. At first glance these seem like reasonable solutions, but closer scrutiny may prove otherwise.

More W2 income is probably not the answer you were looking for. *With job income, the more you make, the more you are taxed; until you eventually invoke the law of diminishing returns.* Additionally, how do you value the extra time you have to spend away from your loved ones? That is time you will never get back. Yes, you may really need more income; but 1099 income pays so much less in taxes and allows lots of tax deductions.

Let me close by saying that sales is not a four-letter word. *Every dollar earned in America comes directly or indirectly from someone at some time selling something to someone.* Even if you work for a nonprofit or government agency, your salary is paid from donations, grants or taxes... all of which are paid from someone's profits from sales.

It's okay to be a little uncomfortable with selling products and services; that puts you in the *overwhelming majority*. But imagine how your finances would improve if you could manage to add this valuable skill to your *income shifting* repertoire. The ability to generate business income will greatly increase the speed with which you can build wealth and acquire assets. You may not be ready for sales yet; but when you are, that option will always be there.

Yes, I realize that there are supposed to be three steps to the **Three Steps To Financial Success**, and that we have only covered two so far. However, *Step Three: Build Investment Income* is so significant that it warrants a chapter all to itself.

NOTES

CHAPTER 5

BUILD INVESTMENT INCOME

"An investment in knowledge pays
the best interest."

BENJAMIN FRANKLIN

The third and final step to the **Three Steps To Financial Success** is *Build Investment Income*. To put things in perspective, the *poorest* Americans earn 100% of their income from working a job. Conversely, the *wealthiest* Americans earn 100% of their income from investments. *The rest of us fall somewhere in between.* The ultimate goal of Income Shifting is to shift your income from the highest tax bracket to the lowest tax bracket. *Investment income is that lowest tax bracket.*

STEP THREE: Build Investment Income

It was a long road to get you here. We started with W2 employees, who make up over 90% of the workforce, and who have been shackled with every single tax disadvantage possible. In order to effectively counteract some of the downsides of job income, we elected to "launder" some of our income through a homebased business; thus enabling us to keep more of our own hard-earned money and create new cashflow.

A Prospectus is a formal legal document that is required by and filed with the Securities and Exchange Commission (SEC) that provides details about an investment offering for sale to the public.

By utilizing tax savings to accelerate debt elimination, you create yet another new source of cashflow with which to build investment income. Investment income is the best of all worlds. It pays the lowest tax rate, and it benefits from the most powerful economic force on Earth: compound interest. Your investments work tirelessly for you 24/7/365. They never sleep, get sick or go away on vacation. Investment in appreciating assets is your best option for outpacing inflation; particularly those that are income producing as well.

Never confuse investing with saving. You save by simply not spending, or by depositing money in a bank that pays you less in interest than the rate of inflation. *While investing does come with a certain amount of risk; much of that risk can be managed if not completely mitigated.* Saved money will be worth much less in the future than it is right now. Properly managed, investments should appreciate because money making money is a wealth building machine.

What Is A Cashflow Strategist?

Disclaimer alert. I am not a licensed CPA or certified financial advisor. It is not my intent to give you investment advice. I am a *"cashflow strategist."* I teach financial strategies, and help demystify for laymen how money really works in America. I will not advise you what to invest in or who to invest with. *My goal is to help you find the money to invest, and then encourage you to seek out a qualified professional to advise you.*

I will, however recommend to you a couple of things that need to happen before you even begin to think about investing. First, you need to use the strategies you have learned so far to lower your taxes, eliminate your revolving debt and become debt free. If you still have debt, then part of everything you earn will be lost. It's like taking two steps forward and one step back.

Next, you should use the cashflow from tax and debt savings to start an *Emergency Fund.* As you know, sometimes life happens; and when it does, you will need access to a stash of liquid

Black Income Shifters

MONEY MANAGER INVEST THE
FUND'S CAPITAL AND
ATTEMPT TO PRODUCE
CAPITAL GAINS AND INCOME
FOR THE FUND'S INVESTORS.

and/or semi-liquid cash. Depending on your lifestyle, the amount needed will vary. Ideally your emergency fund should be invested with money managers who will pay you

A Mutual Fund is an investment vehicle made up of a pool of funds collected from many investors for the purpose of investing in securities such as stocks, bonds, money market instruments and similar assets.

interest higher than the rate of inflation; while simultaneously allowing you access to your money within twenty four to forty eight hours.

If you are fortunate enough to have an employer provided retirement plan, I encourage you to max that out with voluntary contributions before you begin investing on your own. If you have a 401k that allows an employer match, max that option out first. If there is a supplemental benefit such as a 403b that allows additional unmatched investment, go to that next; if no such option exists, an IRA could be a good alternative. Income Shifting can provide the seed money needed to get started.

That being said, you can't even begin to understand investments, if you don't speak the language. And, by design, the language is complicated and difficult to understand. The intent is to intimidate you into believing that finance is beyond your capacity to comprehend, and that you need to hire a professional for even the most rudimentary of tasks.

This simply isn't true. Should you consult with a qualified CPA or financial advisor on major decisions? Of course; but don't make the mistake of selling yourself short.

You Must Talk The Talk

Once you understand the terminology, the veil of secrecy is lifted. For example, there are four general categories of investments:

1. Cash Equivalents
2. Bonds
3. Stocks
4. Real Assets

Each has its own advantages and disadvantages combined with a certain degree of risk. Your specific financial needs at a particular time will determine which option or options work best for you. Once you have money to invest, this is where a financial advisor can be helpful.

Cash Equivalents are the form of investment that you may be most familiar with. They are typically offered by banks, brokerage firms and the government. The most common options are *CDs, passbook savings accounts, money market accounts,* etc. They are attractive to people who are *risk adverse,* offering safety and guarantees in exchange for very low return on investment. In fact, *the money you invest here is guaranteed to be worth less when you take it out than when you put it in* because cash equivalents pay you less than the rate of inflation.

A **Bond** is, basically, a loan to a federal, municipal or corporate entity that finances a specific or particular type of project. When you or I, for example, need money, we have to take out a loan. A municipality, like a state, would float a bond. *A bond pays you its face value at a specified rate of interest on its maturity date, usually ten years or more.* Another way to look at it is that a bond is just a loan packaged as an investment. Variations include a **note**, which matures in 2 years or less, and a **bill** which matures in 1 year or less. *A good thing to know about bonds is that as the prime interest rate increases, bond value decreases…* and vice versa.

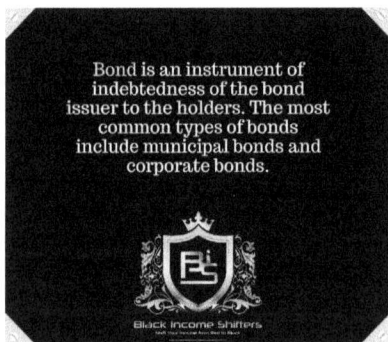

Bond is an instrument of indebtedness of the bond issuer to the holders. The most common types of bonds include municipal bonds and corporate bonds.

Black Income Shifters

With **Stocks**, you are buying part ownership in a company. It's that simple. Your investment rises or falls with the financial performance of the company. However, there are many different types of stocks. Terminology plays a part here, as well. A *dividend stock* pays out income to stockholders periodically. While a *growth stock* reinvests its profits back into the business; hopefully, increasing the value of the stock. When a stock appreciates in value, this is known as *capital gains*. A stock can either appreciate or depreciate, and its true value is realized at the time it is sold or traded.

Mutual Funds are another option to consider. Investing in individual stocks and bonds can be very risky for the inexperienced investor, so *mutual funds* are a good alternative that allows professional money managers to manage groups of stocks and/or bonds on your behalf. This is exactly what the banks do with your money. They depend on money managers like Vanguard, Fidelity and T. Rowe Price to invest your money and earn them 8% to 12%... then they pay you 1%. And they didn't even buy you dinner first!

Real Assets, in the form of precious metals, commodities, real estate and private business are where the big returns are. *Ninety percent of millionaires are made from investing in real assets*. It is possible to make, or lose, a lot of money quickly with real assets. It may surprise you to see private business listed as a real asset. If you have ever seen the TV show, Shark Tank, notice

A Stock is a share in the ownership of a company. Stock represents a claim on the company's assets and earnings.

that the billion dollar investors are investing in businesses. This is where the real money is made, no pun intended.

You may be even more surprised to learn that a homebased business is also a real asset. The potential for unlimited income is there; however, its true value to employees is in the guaranteed tax deductions. Particularly in the first few years, most people will generate more cashflow from tax savings than from product sales. Even a business that is losing money can still be an asset because of the day to day tax deductions and other advantages. Real estate, on the other hand, can become a liability if it loses value and you do not have the resources to ride out the economic downturn.

I'm going to stop here. This chapter was not intended to make you an investment expert; only to give you a basic understanding of investment terminology and strategy so that you can be purposeful in your selection of a financial advisor. Don't let them baffle you with baloney, or convince you that this stuff is so complicated that you should just let them handle it.

How many broke former millionaire athletes and entertainers did just that?

NOTES

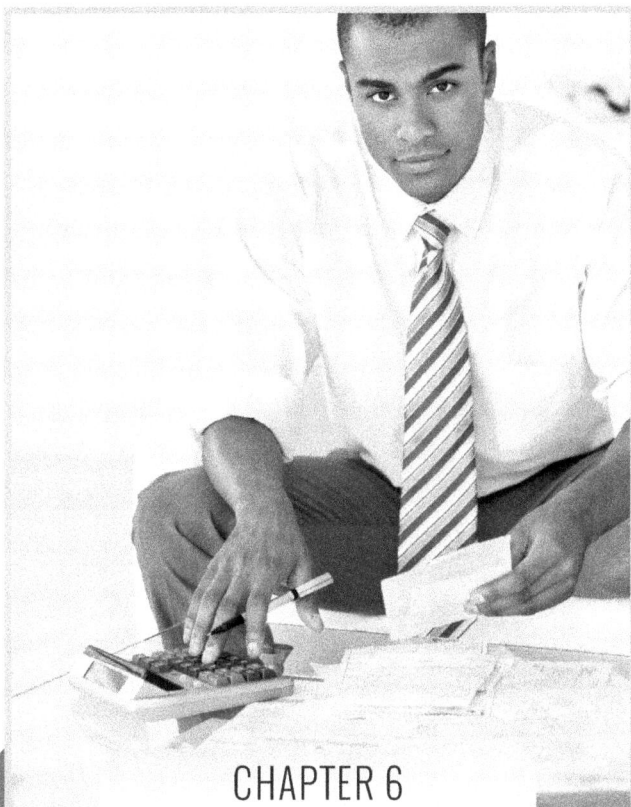

CHAPTER 6

THE JOB ISN'T OVER UNTIL THE PAPERWORK IS DONE

"When the student is ready, the teacher will appear."

CHINESE PROVERB

Knowledge without application is an illusion. What good does it do to have all this information about money and how it really works in America, and not have a game plan for its implementation? At no time in our history is financial education needed more than it is today. This is why the **Income Shifters Academy** was created.

The *Academy* was purposefully designed to foster economic empowerment, and to guide you step by step through your transition from *consumer* to *producer*. This course will show you how to find the money you need by generating new cashflow from the money you already make.

Once you learn how to create new cashflow by minimizing your taxes and debt, generating tax deductions, earning 1099 income, and getting passive income from investments; you will be in charge of your finances for, perhaps, the first time in your life.

As an *Academy* participant, you will receive

regular instruction in the form of videos, webinars, documents, reading assignments and real world application. Also included in your enrollment fee are three thirty minute, one on one personal coaching sessions with a faculty advisor.

Nothing theoretical here, this is as real as it gets. You will earn *real* money, write off *real* expenses, keep *real* tax records and create new cashflow with which to pay bills, invest or simply improve your quality of life. Be careful, though; the risk is real as well.

Déjà Vu All Over Again

Your Academy training begins with instruction in how to correctly adjust your *W4 Tax Withholding Form*. Over 80% of Americans fill it out incorrectly, causing us to overpay our taxes by having too much tax withheld from our paychecks. Failure to correct your W4 can leave, literally, thousands of dollars on the table.

Another reason we begin with the W4 is strictly psychological. Correcting your W4 is the fastest and easiest way to take back your hard-earned tax money from Uncle Sam and see some additional money in your paycheck right away. There is nothing like cold, hard cash to make a point.

The average monthly paycheck increase typically ranges from $200 to $400 a month ($2,400 to $4,800 annually); but I have seen increases of $800 per month or more.

If you continue to claim "zero or one allowance" on your W4 so that you don't owe taxes at the end of the year; you have the most to gain by completing the worksheets and discovering what your correct number of allowances should be. That way, you can at least make an informed decision.

Should you miscalculate and end up owing a couple of hundred dollars at tax time, it's not the end of the world. As long as you pay it off with your tax return, you have actually done to Uncle Sam what he has been doing to you for years... *borrowed his money interest free for a year and used it to pay your bills, lower your debt and invest.* Now that's what I call irony.

The W4 is two pages long (front and back) and consists of a *Personal Allowances Worksheet, Employee's Withholding Allowance Certificate,* a *Deductions and Adjustments Worksheet,* and also a *Two-Earners Multiple Jobs Worksheet.* There is no set number of allowances for every person or situation. This is why it is important to read each question a on both pages and answer them honestly. It is the only way to determine the most correct number of allowances for you and your situation.

I would lay odds that most people reading this are only familiar with the section of *Page 1* called the *Employee's Personal Allowances Certificate*. That's the little stub on the bottom of the front page where you list how many allowances you wish to claim.

If you are a single parent with kids, are head of household, pay for child care and claim the Child Care Credit; then *Page 1* can be a gold mine of allowances for you. However, if you are single, with no dependents and no mortgage, you would be hard-pressed to come away from page one with more than a couple.

Page 2 can open up a whole new world of opportunities to generate new allowances. The first question on the *Deductions and Adjustments Worksheet* gives you the opportunity to write off your home mortgage interest, state and local taxes, and certain medical expenses. If, for example you were able to justify $20,000 of expense here, you could claim an additional four to five more allowances.

To put this in perspective, for my clients, an allowance has been worth from $500 to $1,000 annually. There are multiple factors that go into the value of an allowance for an individual, so this is not an exact science. However, it does give you an idea of how a few extra allowances can make a difference.

Question #1 is a great resource for people with mortgages, but for others, not so much. But don't despair, there is always *Question #4*. This is where qualified individuals get to write off thousands of dollars in everyday lifestyle expenses like your cell phone, laptop, internet service, eating out, travel, auto mileage, etc. These are things you are going to spend money on anyway, so why not write them off?

Under the right circumstances, it is possible for some people to generate double digits in W4 allowances. I would recommend caution here. Some states require employers to report to the IRS any employee who claims ten or more allowances on their W4. Even though I could legitimately claim more than ten allowances, I choose not to do so. I always make it my practice to stay off the IRS' radar screen as much as possible.

A W4 demonstration video will be provided to you as part of the Academy curriculum; demonstrating line by line how to correctly fill out your W4. As an Academy participant, you are provided with two one-on-one coaching sessions. This might be a good time to cash them in for a little coaching support. It is important that you thoroughly understand how this works. There are people in your life that will need your guidance.

While you don't necessarily need a homebased business in order to derive benefit from correcting your W4; the impact is minimal when compared to being able to proportionately write off most of your lifestyle as a business expense. For employees, the primary benefit of a homebased business is in the potential for business tax deductions.

The Right Tool For The Job

The key is in *documentation*. The IRS requires *good tax recordkeeping* in order to claim tax deductions. There is nothing more frustrating than having a legitimate tax deduction nullified during an audit simply because you failed to document properly.

There was a time, and not that long ago either, when asking the average person to keep accurate tax record and document all relevant expenses would have been a monumental task. Those with resources would simply hire someone to do it; those without resources just wouldn't do it at all, leaving thousands of their hard earned tax money on the table each year.

Today, however, there are many simple, easy to use financial software packages on the market that make this task palatable. I personally recommend a proprietary software known as the **Cashflow Manager**. I literally use it every day to track my deductible expenses such as auto mileage, cell phone, eating out, travel, entertainment, etc.; as well as my personal expenses like medical copays, prescriptions, and other eligible non-reimbursed expenses.

The *Cashflow Manager* comes with a handy smart phone app that allows you to take on the spot photos of your receipts, attach them to your expense records and store them in the cloud so that no storage space on your device is used. The software is very easy to use, and comes with an instructional video that explains its basic set up and operation.

But best of all, a *free 30-day trial of the Cashflow Manager software is provided for Academy participants* so that they may experiment in a real world environment. In just a few weeks, you will be surprised at just how quickly all those little tax deductions add up. Once you see the end results of your efforts, motivating you to keep good tax records will not be a problem.

The *Academy* will provide detailed instruction on identifying which of the most common tax deductions are most beneficial to you, and will guide you through the process of effectively utilizing business tax deductions, documenting them, then converting the expense to W4 allowances.

NOTES

CHAPTER 7

HOW TAX DEDUCTIONS REALLY WORK

"A tax loophole is something that benefits the other guy. When it benefits you, it is called tax reform."

RUSSELL B. LONG

How much "cash in your pocket" is a tax deduction really worth? Unlike tax credits, tax deductions are *not* a dollar-for-dollar exchange; instead they reflect a savings of the potential tax you would have paid. *A $1,000 tax deduction, for example, does not put $1,000 back in your pocket.* If you are in a 30% tax bracket, it would actually return around $300 dollars to you.

Tax deductions are calculated taking variables into consideration such as your tax bracket and whether it is W-2, 1099, or investment income that is involved.

> *The advantage of tax deductions is that they reduce your amount of taxable income, which translates into you paying less tax—putting more cash in your pocket. Having a homebased business is not all about earning more income; it is also about making less of your job income taxable."*

Tax deductions create new cashflow by converting many of your expenses; money you were going to spend anyway, into W4 allowances.

Let's not forget about *credits,* though. Not everyone qualifies because they are based on income level; however, those who qualify should take full advantage of them. The most common, and one of the most lucrative, is the Child Care Credit. It makes its appearance on Page 1, Line G of the W4 Tax Withholding Form

I have had single parent clients with two or more eligible dependent children claim 4 to 6 additional allowances based on this credit alone. That represents a lot of money in their paychecks. The mistake often made is to wait until tax refund time to get your money instead of claiming it each month through W4 allowances.

As part of the Academy curriculum, you will get hands on experience with claiming the most common business deductions, documenting them, converting them to W4 allowances and actually seeing more money in your monthly paycheck. Following are a few examples of deductions you will master:

Auto Mileage Deduction. One of the most beneficial tax deductions available is the *auto mileage deduction.* A day does not go by that you don't hear someone complain about the high price of gasoline. In my area, it currently fluctuates

RICK HOPKINS & ODESSA HOPKINS

between $3.50 and $4.00 a gallon. Let's put this in perspective:

- If you have a 20-gallon tank, it would cost you around $80 to fill up your gas tank.
- If you got 20 miles per gallon, you would be able to drive 400 miles on a tank of gas.
- This equates to about 20 cents a mile that you would pay for gas under these circumstances.
- The current IRS standard mileage reimbursement rate is 55 cents a mile (soon to be 57.5 cents).
- That means that you make 35 cents profit for every mile you drive for business purposes.

Another way to look at it is that Uncle Sam pays you $35 profit for every 100 miles you drive for business purposes. If, for example, you drive 20,000 miles this year; and half of those can be considered business miles— that's a $3,500 tax deduction! The key to making the mileage deduction work for you is to translate trips you would take *anyway* into business miles.

Don't drive extra miles just to have something to write off, that would be counterproductive. You would actually be spending more than you would save. Again, this strategy is completely legal and is recognized and accepted by the IRS as long as it is done with *integrity* and *transparency*. How is this accomplished? I am glad you asked.

> *Suppose during one of your routine trips to run errands, you decided to meet a friend at a restaurant for lunch. Instead of limiting your conversation to the usual mindless chitchat, you tell your friend about your homebased business and how it helps you lower your taxes and debt and build business and retirement income. Voila! Your casual lunch just became a business lunch, and 50% of it can be deducted.*

> *Or maybe you are dining out alone and you just happen to strike up a conversation with the person at the table next to you, or with someone as you are waiting in line to be seated. Talk about your business venture, give them a business card (be sure to get theirs for documentation of the meeting, or at least get their name and contact information), and you have once again created a deductible business expense.*

I cannot overemphasize the importance of documentation and good tax recordkeeping. You need to make it a habit to capture the name of the person you met or ate with, keep a copy of the meal receipt, and record your starting and ending auto mileage in order to have bullet-proof documentation to support your claim. The better you get at transforming everyday expenses into business deductions, the more of your hard-earned tax dollars you can reclaim. Take back your tax!

Business Travel Deduction. If you love to travel, and who doesn't, then you should definitely learn how to write off trips and vacations. If you own rental real estate, you are probably aware that you can write off transportation, food, and other costs related to visiting, maintaining and checking on your property. The *business travel deduction* works much the same way.

It is easy to turn a vacation cruise into a business trip. For example, just allocate some of the time on the ship, or on the island, or at dinner, or at the show to discuss your business. Be sure to collect names and contact information on the people you discussed business with, keep receipts from the trip, or set up a business meeting with a prospective client at your destination point. Just remember to document, document, document; it is worth the effort.

Your homebased business allows you to proportionately claim all necessary expenses during the travel experience. That includes the following:

- *Travel by air, bus, car, cab, train, or other vehicle between your home and the business destination*
- *All expenses incurred by your personal vehicle while you were at a business destination, including tolls, parking meters, and gas*
- *Any food that you need during your trip*
- *Any accommodation that you need during your trip*
- *All tips given to staff during travel*
- *All dry cleaning and laundry bills*
- *Phone calls during your business trip*

It is not unusual to spend $2,000 to $4,000 or more on a vacation trip. If that same trip were claimed as a business trip, again assuming a 30% tax rate, $600 to $1,200 dollars would find its way back to you through tax savings. If you were going to take this trip anyway, that is $600 to $1,200 dollars that can go into _your_ pocket instead of Uncle Sam's. The beauty of this deduction is that you were going to take this trip or vacation anyway.

Hire Your Child Deduction. If you are a parent who pays his child a weekly or monthly allowance, it might surprise you to know just how much this actually costs you. If you really want a cold slap in the face, just calculate how much you need to earn, before taxes, in order to pay that allowance. It is easy to do—just add approximately 30% to what you pay your child in allowance. Are you mad yet? *Well don't get mad; get a homebased business! I know that doesn't rhyme—but I think you get the point.*

First of all, don't you have better things to do with 30% of your hard earned money than to willingly give it to Uncle Sam? How about putting it away in a college fund for your child's future education or using it to pay down your credit card balances? Your business allows you to shield that income from excessive taxation by giving you a vehicle to hire your six- to eighteen-year-old child and pay him/ her a *salary* instead of an allowance—up to $6,200 a year per child! That's right, you can legally do this. IRS rules and regulations apply, of course.

To take advantage of this significant but seldom utilized tax deduction, simply develop a job description for your new "employee" with real responsibilities that are applicable to your business and within the capabilities of your child. Be sure that the job pays a reasonable wage based on those responsibilities.

> *For example, a pre-teen is certainly capable of opening your mail, answering your business line, posting regularly to your social media accounts, performing clerical duties, and researching*

information online.

This is not a game—so this strategy is not to be taken lightly. It can put real money back in your pocket; but, again, transparency and documentation are required by the IRS in order to protect you from being accused of fraud. For example, it will be necessary to set up a separate bank account in which to deposit the funds paid to your child. Make sure there is a clear and transparent paper trail when the money is withdrawn from the account.

Please—do not get caught with your hand in the cookie jar on this one! If you think all this sounds like too much trouble, perhaps this deduction is not for you. However, before you throw the baby out with the bath water, just take a minute and do the math—you may change your mind.

Meals & Entertainment Deduction. If you eat out or attend *concerts, fine arts* or *sporting events*; this is an excellent deduction. Personally, I eat out way too much, but when I do, I make sure to discuss my business and hand out a couple of business cards while I am there. I have actually found new clients this way; but primarily, I am now able to deduct 50% of the cost of the meal and my round trip mileage to and from the restaurant.

This deduction really comes in handy when you

are picking up the check for a meal with several friends and colleagues. From a business standpoint, discussing what you do with others is the foundation of success in this country. Even if the person you talk to is not interested, you never know who they may share your information with.

Communications Deduction. You probably have a *cell phone*, a *laptop* and/or an *internet* connection. All of these are deductible *to the extent that they apply to your business*. It is very important to pay attention to percentages and proportionate usage. Don't claim 100% of your personal cell phone, for example. I'm sure you make plenty of personal calls, Facebook posts and tweets on it. The same applies to your laptop and internet.

Be reasonable with Uncle Sam and he will be reasonable with you. Claiming write offs is equal parts good faith and documentation. Don't be so intent on avoiding all contact with the IRS that you are not willing to claim tax advantages you are rightfully entitled to. The keys to dealing with the IRS are to be truthful, operate in good faith and keep good tax records.

"Visit the IRS Website at www.irs.gov/credits-deductions for Business Deductions and Requirements. To ensure you maximize allowable deductions, provide all receipts and records to your accountant or tax preparer."

NOTES

CHAPTER 8

HOW DO I BUILD WEALTH?

"Expect the best. Prepare for the
worst. Capitalize on what comes."

ZIG ZIGLAR

Strategy, above all else, should direct your efforts to build generational wealth for you and your family. Once you know what it is that you want to accomplish, you can begin to put together a strategy that will get you there. Strategy, like most things in this world, comes in two varieties: *"do it yourself"* or *"done for you."* There is merit in either, but why reinvent the wheel if it isn't necessary.

If you play chess, you understand that no move is a bad move... if it is made with a well thought out strategy in mind. A king's pawn opening is just as strong as a queen's pawn opening in the hands of a master strategist. Wealth does not happen by accident. It happens because someone, at some time, had a plan to be wealthy and executed it.

Once wealth is created, if properly managed, it can be passed on from generation to generation. This is the goal of the *Income Shifters Academy.* We want to share financial strategies and help you develop your own wealth plan. Admittedly, planning is usually not a lot of fun. I think you will agree that it is fun to generate new cashflow without working longer hours, getting a second job, begging your boss for a raise; or having to sell products or recruit people.

Fail To Plan, Plan To Fail

As an Academy participant, you will work hands-on to develop your own specific, task driven, measurable wealth plan with pre-determined deliverables based on real dollars. Stephen R. Covey, in his book *The Seven Habits of Highly Effective People* says that "you should begin with the end in mind;" and we will do just that. As we begin the planning process, you will be asked several baseline questions that will guide your planning process:

- What year, at the latest, do you plan to retire?
- What is the least amount of monthly income you require at retirement?
- How much monthly retirement income do you expect to receive from all sources? (Such as Social Security, company pensions, 401k, 403b, etc.)

If you are like most people, unless you are nearing retirement age, you probably have not put actual numbers to these questions.

For someone in their twenties or thirties, it can be difficult to think much about retirement; it just seems so far off in the future. But then you blink; and now you are in your fifties wishing you had prepared better when you were younger. It is important that you know exactly what year you want to retire and how much income you need, because if you come up short, you may not be able to retire after all. Be sure to factor in time and inflation.

If you are living on $6,000 a month now, you will need more than $6,000 to maintain your same standard of living if your retirement date is many years away. If you know how much you need to live on, but your current investment portfolio will not produce that amount, you need to know that now... while you still have time to do something about it.

Increasingly more and more Americans will have to work a job until the day they die because they failed to have and to execute a viable retirement plan. Based on how you answer these and other questions our software will calculate what year you will reach your retirement income goal based on your current lifestyle, spending and investing habits.

Don't be surprised if it takes you several years longer than you expect... unless you can find ways to increase revenue, reduce expenses, minimize taxes and eliminate debt. Remember your *Financial Enemies* will still be hard at work making it difficult for you to succeed... in this case, especially *inflation*. Unless you are able to outpace inflation with your retirement investments, assuming you are able to hit your income target, it will have much less buying power.

When we speak of someone being on a *fixed income*, we often assume the subject is a senior. The fact is, if you are limited to job income alone, you are on a fixed income. This makes it difficult to accurately plan for retirement because life is not fixed, it is a moving target. The security of having a steady paycheck; of knowing exactly how much you have coming in at any given time has its advantages. Except for when life zigs instead of zags.

Investment income primarily funds your retirement; however much of its financial performance is out of your control. This is why you need the other two forms of cashflow provided by your homebased business: *business tax deductions* and *1099 income*. Unlike your job income, either or both can be ramped up if needed. When your wealth plan requires you to generate more cashflow, your business, not your job, is where you can find it.

Be A Cashflow Strategist

The **Cashflow Strategist** software will guide you through setting up a prioritized debt elimination plan that will show you how to pay off credit cards and other high interest revolving interest loans in a few months instead of years. It will also address larger loans like auto loans, and long term debt such as mortgages. It will help you identify, prioritize and track all of your recurring expenses.

For your part, the planning process is mostly just *plug and play*. The software does most of the work. You will have some hard choices to make, but they will mostly concern having the discipline to regularly monitor your plan's progress, and make the necessary corrections in order to stay on course. Implementing the plan is important, but can be tedious; so don't forget to have a little fun on your journey to financial success.

You should probably reevaluate your *Cashflow Strategist Personal Financial Plan* annually.

NOTES

CHAPTER 9

HOW TO CHOOSE YOUR HBB

"Stay committed to your decisions, but
stay flexible in your approach."

TONY ROBBINS

The world as we know it has changed drastically since the onset of the Information Age. The non-traditional has replaced the traditional. The innovative has replaced the tried and true. Perhaps you are fortunate enough <u>not</u> to have had your job rendered obsolete by technology and automation. Many are not so lucky.

However, if the unthinkable were to happen, and you unexpectedly lost your job, do you have a *"Plan B"* in place to help you survive? Most do not. Remember that over 90% of Americans earn 100% of their income from a job. This is the equivalent of putting all of your eggs in one basket. Limiting yourself to only one stream of income is never a good financial strategy.

Someone understood that virtual business would someday outperform its traditional brick and mortar counterpart. Someday has arrived. Examples are all around you. The country's largest transportation company, *Uber*, doesn't own a single vehicle. Walmart is no longer our nation's largest retailer; that distinction now falls to *Amazon.com*.

And the world's largest hotel company, *Airbnb*, doesn't own a single building.

Bank tellers have been replaced by ATMs, and fast food workers will be the next victims of advancing technology; not to mention the manufacturing jobs that have been automated or shipped overseas. Employees find themselves operating without a safety net, as far as their jobs are concerned.

For example, at my company, standard language in each employment offer letter reads: "Your employment is 'at will.' This means that either you or the company may terminate the employment relationship at any time, for any reason or without reason."

Did you ever wonder why Uncle Sam is so generous with allowing so many tax advantages for homebased businesses? Doesn't that unnecessarily drain funds from the IRS tax coffers? Is he helping you out of the goodness of his heart? Is this his attempt to introduce some fairness to the tax codes? Of course, the last two questions were rhetorical.

I would propose that rather than pay you unemployment insurance or public assistance, Uncle Sam would prefer to pay you to operate a part time homebased business; one that could possibly be ramped up to full time should you lose your job or otherwise be unable to work. Regardless of intent, I see this as a win/win scenario.

I would strongly recommend that every employee take full advantage of these rare opportunities to benefit from loopholes in the tax codes. After all, it isn't every day that Uncle Sam puts laws in place that lighten the employee's tax burden.

This is why homebased business ownership is at the heart of the *Income Shifting Strategy*. So, at this point, the only question is what kind of homebased business is right for you? It is said that if you love what you do, you will never work a day in your life. I have been blessed to find a career that has been so for me. Conversely, I have friends who literally hate their jobs and the people they work with. I pity them.

Keep this in mind when selecting a homebased business for yourself. There are nearly as many different types of homebased businesses as there are people who own them. There are some very basic requirements to qualify; primarily, you must devote three to four hours a week to your business with the intent to make a profit.

Choose Your Weapon

Not every business makes a profit right away. *Black*

Enterprise Magazine, one of the top publications of its kind, took six years before finally becoming profitable. Most homebased businesses, and businesses in general, are not profitable initially. In fact in the first few years of operation, a business is likely to generate more cashflow through tax deductions than through product sales.

Some examples of traditional homebased businesses are doctor's, dentist's and lawyer's offices. Obviously, this is a very select few. Others have taken hobbies and turned them into businesses. I have a very good friend who is a manager at a power company; but also is an excellent artist. He sells his paintings online, and qualifies for business tax deductions.

The most popular, however, is direct sales, sometimes known as *network marketing.* Network marketing is a mixed bag. More women millionaires have been created through network marketing than any other industry worldwide. Anyone can be successful in network marketing; but ultimately, many more fail than succeed. This is not the fault of the industry, but of the human condition.

We are willing to work extremely hard for years at a traditional job for low wages; yet expect to become millionaires with a part time business in six months. There are good network marketing companies and bad ones; just as there are good traditional companies and bad. Scams have been perpetrated through network marketing companies, just as scams have been perpetrated through traditional companies. Many times those who blame *pyramid schemes* and the like for their lack of success, simply did not work hard enough to be successful.

Just as I will not give you investment advice, I also will not tell you what kind of homebased business to start. I will, however, share with you some of the thoughts that helped me make my own decision. Don't expect to get it exactly right the first time. I failed several times before I found the right fit; but when I finally found it, the game changed for me.

I am very uncomfortable selling products and recruiting people. Ironically, my first homebased business was in direct sales. I was introduced to a product that was so good that I was sure that everyone I knew would want to buy it too... I was wrong! It is definitely a great product; I still use it today, but I was not the one to sell it. The problem wasn't the product or the company, it was me.

I will spare you my other failures, and skip to my ultimate success. When I finally found the right company for me; one where being a master salesperson was not required, everything changed. All of a sudden, people who said *no* before, were now saying *yes*. People who complained about cost, were now swiping their credit cards. I had found the right fit.

That "right fit" homebased business is out there for you as well. As an employee, the economic deck is stacked against you. Don't misunderstand me; a good job is a blessing, but it will not make you wealthy by itself. The system will not allow it. The more you make, the more the IRS takes; unless you protect your income from excessive taxation, eliminate your debt and build investment income.

The concept of *Income Shifting* changed my life, and the way I think about money forever. It opened my eyes to how I could begin to *participate* in our capitalistic economy, instead of just contributing my hard-earned money to it. This knowledge and new-found confidence paved the way for the founding of the *Income Shifters Academy*.

Successful businesses all have one thing in common. They identified a problem and solved it. The Academy has done just that. Most people do not like to sell products. Most people are skeptical about network marketing opportunities. We simply cannot envision ourselves as business owners. The school system prepared us to be employees, not employers.

Not everyone can sell; but anyone can save money on taxes, eliminate debt, claim business deductions, and create passive income through investments. In order to do this, however, you must have a homebased business. There is no way around it… embrace it. The academy will educate you on financial strategies and make you more comfortable executing them.

Business Is Business

So how do you go about choosing a homebased business that is right for you? My suggestions would be:

- *Choose a Business You Love*. Perhaps you *settled* for your job only because you had obligations. Don't make that mistake again.

- *Choose a Business That You Are Good At*. Nothing breeds success like success.

- *Do Your Homework*. Not all homebased businesses are created equal. There really are scams out there. Choose wisely.

- *Study the Compensation Plan*. It is important

to understand the details of how you get paid. Some comp plans can be intentionally complex and confusing. Do the math.

- *Culture of Support.* Coaching and mentoring is necessary in business just as it is on your job. If you get the feeling that you are on your own... you probably are.

A brief discussion on the different business classifications is appropriate here. I would suggest that you obtain an E.I.N number. An E.I.N is to a business what a S.S.N. is to an individual. It allows Uncle Sam to identify and track your business income and expenses; just as its counterpart identifies and tracks your personal ones. You can apply online at <u>www.irs.gov</u>. It is free and only takes a few minutes.

When you apply for your E.I.N., you will need to choose a business name and business classification. I would suggest that you go with a generic business name to allow for maximum flexibility. For example, the name, *Smith Paint Store* is specific; whereas, *Smith Enterprises,* allows for more wiggle room.

Your business classification, on the other hand, requires much more thought. Choose carefully, based on your needs; but also taking into account the amount of risk involved. The basic classifications are:

1. *Sole Proprietorship*. The sole proprietorship is the simplest classification under which one can operate a business. It is not a legal entity. It simply refers to a person who owns the business and is personally responsible for its debts.

2. *Partnership*. A partnership is a single business where two or more people share ownership. Each partner contributes to all aspects of the business, including money, property, labor or skill. In return, each partner shares in the profits and losses of the business.

3. *Limited Liability Corporation*. It is a business structure that combines the pass-through taxation of a partnership or sole proprietorship with the limited liability of a corporation. An LLC is not a corporation; it is a legal form of a company that provides limited liability to its owners in many jurisdictions.

4. *Corporation*. The Corporation is, by far, the most complex business form. So much so, in fact, that it goes well beyond the scope of this text.

Another advantage of a network marketing homebased business is that the parent company bears the burden of dealing with most of the legal issues. You operate as an independent associate; basically, as an independent contractor/business owner. As such, you are not required to have an E.I.N.; you can use your S.S.N. instead.

You can operate as a Sole Proprietorship and continue to use your S.S.N.; or use an E.I.N. if you prefer. As a rule of thumb, you may still want to consider getting an E.I.N. because it lessens the exposure of your S.S.N. in cyber space.

NOTES

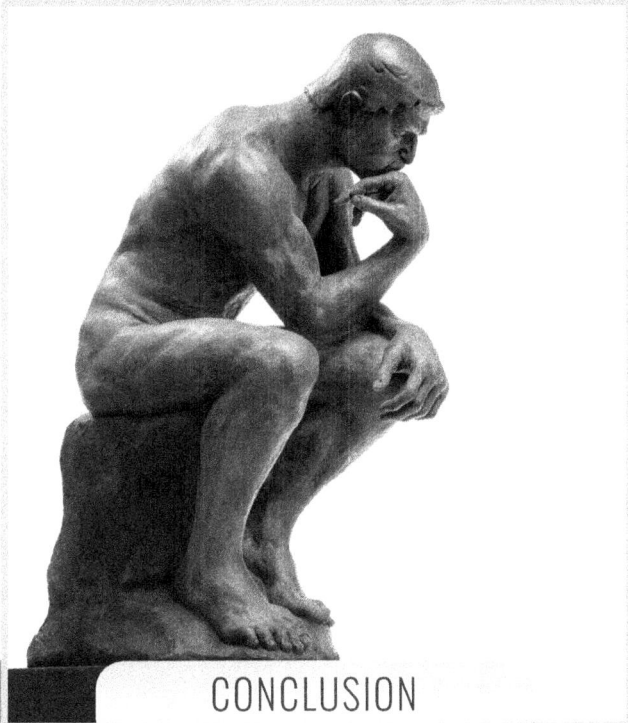

CONCLUSION

2 OBJECTIVES, 4 CHALLENGES AND 3 SOLUTIONS

"Without strategy, execution is aimless.
Without execution, strategy is useless."

MORRIS CHANG

In closing, I propose that everything you have learned from this book can be summarized in one very simple formula: *"2 Objectives + 4 Challenges + 3 Solutions = Financial Success."*

2 Objectives

Objective #1 is to be able to live your desired lifestyle now. This means different things to different people. For some, $50,000 a year is desirable; for others, it may be $500,000 or even $5 million. This is made possible by generating enough cashflow during your working years to provide a comfortable lifestyle for yourself and your family. In other words, your *current lifestyle* is paid for by your *labor*.

Objective #2 is to be able to stop working someday without having to lower your standard of living. This is only possible if you were able to acquire enough revenue producing assets during your working years to maintain your desired lifestyle. Failure to do so may result in having to work a job until the day you die. In other words, your *future lifestyle* is paid for by your *investments*.

4 Challenges

<u>Challenge #1</u> is *High Taxes*. You lose a third of your income to taxes. If you count sales taxes, property taxes and other specialty taxes; it is actually closer to half. This is why Income Shifting starts with showing you how to minimize your taxes. Uncle Sam is going to get his tax money from someone... but he doesn't have to get it all from you.

<u>Challenge #2</u> is Debt. Ironically, most people end up in debt due to trying to compensate for money lost to taxes by taking out credit cards and other high interest loans. This may seem like a good idea at the time; but credit is like a drug. It seems harmless enough at first; but before you know it you are caught in the credit trap, up to your neck in interest debt.

<u>Challenge #3</u> is Inflation. It goes by many names, "the silent income killer," and "death by a thousand cuts" just to name a couple. Inflation doubles every twenty years; so if you are not earning twice as much as you were in 1997, you have not kept pace with inflation. Sadly, your money is worth less now than it was twenty years ago.

Challenge #4 is Inadequate Cashflow Management. In order to efficiently manage your cashflow, you first need cashflow to manage. If you are living paycheck to paycheck, this can be challenging. All that is holding you back is a lack of financial education and, of course, implementation of the financial strategies learned from this book.

3 Solutions

Anyone can point out challenges; but few can offer real solutions. Information is power, and financial education is information on steroids.

Solution #1 is Income Shifting. Keep more of your own money. Use it to make yourself wealthy instead of Uncle Sam, the banks, insurance companies and big business. Take back your tax. Eliminate your debt. Use that new cashflow to begin investing and acquiring assets that produce passive income. Then build generational wealth by teaching your kids to do the same.

Solution #2 is Business Ownership. Business owners participate in capitalism by growing the economy and taking a piece of it for themselves. Employees only contribute their hard earned money to capitalism and get little in return. They pay taxes and buy products; but do not acquire assets and build wealth. Business ownership allows employees to participate in capitalism by being able to shelter their job income with tax deductions, as well as having the option to earn additional tax-advantaged 1099 business income.

Solution #3 is *Build Investment Income.* Investments generate what is known as "passive income." It is the best of all worlds. It pays the lowest tax rate, and your money works for you instead of you working for your money Investments never get sick, tired, sleep or go on vacation. If monitored and managed properly, investments can outpace inflation and provide the cashflow to support you after your working years.

Next Steps...

The ball is in your court now. You have what you need to take back control of your finances and build wealth for yourself and your loved ones. I urge you to not just implement what you have learned; but also to share this information with others... pay it forward, if you will. The true value of knowledge, like a smile, is when you give it away. We are way behind so "each one teach one" is no longer good enough. "Each one teach two" must be our new directive...

www.ingramcontent.com/pod-product-compliance
Lightning Source LLC
Chambersburg PA
CBHW060613200326
41521CB00007B/760